# Maid of Honor Planner

## THIS PLANNER BELONGS TO

......................................................................

## IF FOUND, PLEASE RETURN TO:

Name:

Address:

Cell Phone:                                    FAX:

Work Phone:                                   FAX:

Primary E-Mail:

Secondary E-Mail:

# Content

# Dates to Remember

Wedding Date_____

Save the Dates Mailing By_____

Coordinate Gift Registry_____

Dress Shopping (Bride)_____

Dress Shopping (Bridesmaids)_____

Meeting With Caterer_____

Invitation Mailed By_____

Bridal Shower_____

Final Bridal Alterations_____

Finalize Guest List_____

Bachelorette Party_____

Wedding Day Hair / Nails_____

# Maid of Honor Duties

- [ ] Be available for the bride at all the times.

- [ ] Help the bride shop for her wedding dress & bridesmaid dresses.

- [ ] Attend her dress fittings.

- [ ] Help bride finding vendors and suppliers for the wedding and go with her to meetings and appointments with them, in case required.

- [ ] Offer to help with wedding invitations, and assist with additional wedding projects.

- [ ] Go with her to cake and menu tastings.

- [ ] Oversee and keep track of pre-wedding expenses, help her to stick to the budget.

- [ ] Help with seating plans.

- [ ] Plan and attend the bridal shower and bachelorette party with the bridesmaids.

- [ ] Manage the bridesmaids, and mediate any conflict that may arise.

- [ ] Shop and pay for your own wedding attire.

- [ ] Attend all pre-wedding events, including the wedding rehearsal, & beauty appointments.

- [ ] Be the information point- know all the fine details of the wedding as well as the registry in case guests want ot know something.

- [ ] Help the bride to confirm the bookings- make a master checklist to ensure that nothing has been left out.

- [ ] Manage the bridal party, assign tasks where needed, organize accomodation for wedding party guests who live far away, help organize travel logistics etc.

- [ ] Make sure that everything is pre-planned, so that you can enjoy every celebration without last minute hassles, follow checklist, maintain master to-do list.

- [ ] Help her to pick accessories and wedding attire like shoes, and her veil.
- [ ] Get a Wedding gift.
- [ ] Prepare emergency kit for the bride.
- [ ] Help the bride with her hair, makeup and getting into the dress.
- [ ] Give a toast to the bride and groom at the reception.
- [ ] Hold the bride's bouquet.
- [ ] Act as a cohost at the reception and ensure everything goes as planned.
- [ ] Point the guests to guest book station, favors, gift tables, photobooth.
- [ ] Keep the bride calm on the Big Day, Be a great listener, and moral support for the bride throughout the process.

# Master to-do List

- [ ] _____
- [ ] _____
- [ ] _____
- [ ] _____
- [ ] _____
- [ ] _____
- [ ] _____
- [ ] _____
- [ ] _____
- [ ] _____
- [ ] _____
- [ ] _____
- [ ] _____
- [ ] _____
- [ ] _____
- [ ] _____
- [ ] _____

- [ ] _____
- [ ] _____
- [ ] _____
- [ ] _____
- [ ] _____
- [ ] _____
- [ ] _____
- [ ] _____
- [ ] _____
- [ ] _____
- [ ] _____
- [ ] _____
- [ ] _____
- [ ] _____
- [ ] _____
- [ ] _____
- [ ] _____

# Master to-do List

# Wedding planning Checklist

## 12 Months before the wedding

- ☐ Send an engagement gift or card to the bride.
- ☐ Help bride in finalizing the venue.
- ☐ Help the bride shop for her wedding dress.
- ☐ Help the bride look for bridesmaid dresses.
- ☐ Help the bride look for vendors.
- ☐ Lend a Hand With DIY Projects.
- ☐ Plan a get-together with all the bridesmaids, to encourage bonding.

## 3-6 Months before the wedding

- ☐ Purchase your dress.
- ☐ Start planning Bachelorette Party/ Bridal Shower.
- ☐ Coordinate bridesmaid hair/ makeup.
- ☐ Be familiar with the gift registry.
- ☐ Brainstorm bachelorette party ideas.
- ☐ Plan your hotel accommodation, if wedding venue is out of town.

# Wedding planning Checklist

## 3-4 Months before the wedding

- ☐ Help bride address invites.
- ☐ Book flight, if wedding venue is out of town.
- ☐ Purchase Shoes, Accessories, and Jewelry.

## 2-3 Months before the wedding

- ☐ Throw bridal shower / Bachelorette Party.
- ☐ Schedule alteration appointment for dress.
- ☐ Schedule hair and makeup appointment.
- ☐ Look for wedding gift.
- ☐ Plan your hotel accommodation, if wedding venue is out of town.

## 1-2 Months before the wedding

- ☐ Write Maid of Honor speech.
- ☐ Help the bride with any last minute errands.
- ☐ Help the bride make favors, if needed.

# Wedding planning Checklist

### 1 Month before the wedding

☐ Give the bride moral support as the big day approaches.

☐ Prepare a wedding emergency kit for the bride and bridal party.

☐ Have a wedding weekend checklist and inform all bridesmaids.

### 1 Week before the wedding

☐ Throw bridal shower / Bachelorette Party (If not done yet).

☐ Be familiar with wedding schedule and help delegate tasks to the bridal party.

☐ Keep bridesmaids up to date on plans.

### 1 Day before the Wedding

☐ Attend wedding rehearsal and dinner.

☐ Layout clothing.

# Wedding planning Checklist

## Wedding Day

- ☐ Help Bride get ready.
- ☐ Hold the bride's bouquet during the vow and ring exchange.
- ☐ Help the bride change outfits (if needed).
- ☐ Make sure the bride eats and stays hydrated.
- ☐ Photo shoot.
- ☐ Act as the host – greet guests and direct them to the right places.
- ☐ Have Fun.

## Notes

..............................................................................................

..............................................................................................

..............................................................................................

..............................................................................................

..............................................................................................

..............................................................................................

..............................................................................................

# Vendor Contact

## WEDDING PLANNER

Name: .............................................

Address: ..........................................

.............................................

Phone: ...........................................

Web: ..............................................

Notes: ............................................

.............................................

## RECEPTION VENUE

Name: .............................................

Address: ..........................................

.............................................

Phone: ...........................................

Web: ..............................................

Notes: ............................................

.............................................

## CEREMONY VENUE

Name: .............................................

Address: ..........................................

.............................................

Phone: ...........................................

Web: ..............................................

Notes: ............................................

.............................................

## OFFICIANT

Name: .............................................

Address: ..........................................

.............................................

Phone: ...........................................

Web: ..............................................

Notes: ............................................

.............................................

## PHOTOGRAPHER

Name: .............................................

Address: ..........................................

.............................................

Phone: ...........................................

Web: ..............................................

Notes: ............................................

.............................................

## VIDEOGRAPHER

Name: .............................................

Address: ..........................................

.............................................

Phone: ...........................................

Web: ..............................................

Notes: ............................................

.............................................

# Vendor Contact

## FLORIST

Name: ......................................................

Address: ..................................................

..........................................................

Phone: ...................................................

Web: ......................................................

Notes: ....................................................

..........................................................

## BAKER

Name: ......................................................

Address: ..................................................

..........................................................

Phone: ...................................................

Web: ......................................................

Notes: ....................................................

..........................................................

## CATERER

Name: ......................................................

Address: ..................................................

..........................................................

Phone: ...................................................

Web: ......................................................

Notes: ....................................................

..........................................................

## TRANSPORTATION

Name: ......................................................

Address: ..................................................

..........................................................

Phone: ...................................................

Web: ......................................................

Notes: ....................................................

..........................................................

## DJ/ ENTERTAINMENT

Name: ......................................................

Address: ..................................................

..........................................................

Phone: ...................................................

Web: ......................................................

Notes: ....................................................

..........................................................

## LIGHTING COMPANY

Name: ......................................................

Address: ..................................................

..........................................................

Phone: ...................................................

Web: ......................................................

Notes: ....................................................

..........................................................

# Vendor Contact

## BRIDAL DRESS

Name: ......................................................

Address: ..................................................

..............................................................

Phone: ....................................................

Web: .......................................................

Notes: .....................................................

..............................................................

## MAKEUP ARTIST

Name: ......................................................

Address: ..................................................

..............................................................

Phone: ....................................................

Web: .......................................................

Notes: .....................................................

..............................................................

## HAIR STYLIST

Name: ......................................................

Address: ..................................................

..............................................................

Phone: ....................................................

Web: .......................................................

Notes: .....................................................

..............................................................

## JEWELER

Name: ......................................................

Address: ..................................................

..............................................................

Phone: ....................................................

Web: .......................................................

Notes: .....................................................

..............................................................

## STATIONARY DESIGNER

Name: ......................................................

Address: ..................................................

..............................................................

Phone: ....................................................

Web: .......................................................

Notes: .....................................................

..............................................................

## VENDOR

Name: ......................................................

Address: ..................................................

..............................................................

Phone: ....................................................

Web: .......................................................

Notes: .....................................................

..............................................................

# Vendor Contact

## VENDOR

Name: ..............................................
Address: ..........................................
................................................................
Phone: ............................................
Web: ...............................................
Notes: ............................................
................................................................

## VENDOR

Name: ..............................................
Address: ..........................................
................................................................
Phone: ............................................
Web: ...............................................
Notes: ............................................
................................................................

## VENDOR

Name: ..............................................
Address: ..........................................
................................................................
Phone: ............................................
Web: ...............................................
Notes: ............................................
................................................................

## VENDOR

Name: ..............................................
Address: ..........................................
................................................................
Phone: ............................................
Web: ...............................................
Notes: ............................................
................................................................

## VENDOR

Name: ..............................................
Address: ..........................................
................................................................
Phone: ............................................
Web: ...............................................
Notes: ............................................
................................................................

## VENDOR

Name: ..............................................
Address: ..........................................
................................................................
Phone: ............................................
Web: ...............................................
Notes: ............................................
................................................................

# Bridal party contact list

| MAID/MATRON OF HONOR: | |
|---|---|
| PHONE: | |
| EMAIL: | |
| DRESS SIZE: | |
| SHOE SIZE: | |
| NOTES: | |

| BRIDESMAID: | |
|---|---|
| PHONE: | |
| EMAIL: | |
| DRESS SIZE: | |
| SHOE SIZE: | |
| NOTES: | |

| BRIDESMAID: | |
|---|---|
| PHONE: | |
| EMAIL: | |
| DRESS SIZE: | |
| SHOE SIZE: | |
| NOTES: | |

| BRIDESMAID: | |
|---|---|
| PHONE: | |
| EMAIL: | |
| DRESS SIZE: | |
| SHOE SIZE: | |
| NOTES: | |

| BRIDESMAID: | |
|---|---|
| PHONE: | |
| EMAIL: | |
| DRESS SIZE: | |
| SHOE SIZE: | |
| NOTES: | |

# Bridal party contact list

| BRIDESMAID: | |
|---|---|
| PHONE: | |
| EMAIL: | |
| DRESS SIZE: | |
| SHOE SIZE: | |
| NOTES: | |

| BRIDESMAID: | |
|---|---|
| PHONE: | |
| EMAIL: | |
| DRESS SIZE: | |
| SHOE SIZE: | |
| NOTES: | |

| BRIDESMAID: | |
|---|---|
| PHONE: | |
| EMAIL: | |
| DRESS SIZE: | |
| SHOE SIZE: | |
| NOTES: | |

| BRIDESMAID: | |
|---|---|
| PHONE: | |
| EMAIL: | |
| DRESS SIZE: | |
| SHOE SIZE: | |
| NOTES: | |

| BRIDESMAID: | |
|---|---|
| PHONE: | |
| EMAIL: | |
| DRESS SIZE: | |
| SHOE SIZE: | |
| NOTES: | |

# Bridal party contact list

| BEST MAN: | |
|---|---|
| PHONE: | |
| EMAIL: | |
| DRESS SIZE: | |
| SHOE SIZE: | |
| NOTES: | |

| GROOMSMAN: | |
|---|---|
| PHONE: | |
| EMAIL: | |
| DRESS SIZE: | |
| SHOE SIZE: | |
| NOTES: | |

| GROOMSMAN: | |
|---|---|
| PHONE: | |
| EMAIL: | |
| DRESS SIZE: | |
| SHOE SIZE: | |
| NOTES: | |

| GROOMSMAN: | |
|---|---|
| PHONE: | |
| EMAIL: | |
| DRESS SIZE: | |
| SHOE SIZE: | |
| NOTES: | |

| GROOMSMAN: | |
|---|---|
| PHONE: | |
| EMAIL: | |
| DRESS SIZE: | |
| SHOE SIZE: | |
| NOTES: | |

# Bridal party contact list

| GROOMSMAN: | |
|---|---|
| PHONE: | |
| EMAIL: | |
| DRESS SIZE: | |
| SHOE SIZE: | |
| NOTES: | |

| GROOMSMAN: | |
|---|---|
| PHONE: | |
| EMAIL: | |
| DRESS SIZE: | |
| SHOE SIZE: | |
| NOTES: | |

| GROOMSMAN: | |
|---|---|
| PHONE: | |
| EMAIL: | |
| DRESS SIZE: | |
| SHOE SIZE: | |
| NOTES: | |

| GROOMSMAN: | |
|---|---|
| PHONE: | |
| EMAIL: | |
| DRESS SIZE: | |
| SHOE SIZE: | |
| NOTES: | |

| GROOMSMAN: | |
|---|---|
| PHONE: | |
| EMAIL: | |
| DRESS SIZE: | |
| SHOE SIZE: | |
| NOTES: | |

# Wedding Emergency Kit

## Make-up

- ☐ Mascara
- ☐ Highlighter
- ☐ Powder
- ☐ Eyeshadow
- ☐ Eyeliner
- ☐ Lip Balm
- ☐ Lipstick
- ☐ Compact mirror
- ☐ Tweezers
- ☐ Cotton swabs
- ☐ Deodorant
- ☐ Baby Wipes
- ☐ Toothpaste
- ☐ Toothbrush
- ☐ Perfume
- ☐ Makeup Remover
- ☐ Foundation
- ☐ Eyebrow pencil
- ☐ Lotion
- ☐ Nail polish
- ☐
- ☐
- ☐
- ☐

## Hair Touch-up

- ☐ Straightener
- ☐ Bobby pins
- ☐ Comb
- ☐ Hair Clips/ Ties
- ☐ Brush
- ☐ Curling Iron
- ☐ Hairspray
- ☐
- ☐
- ☐
- ☐
- ☐
- ☐
- ☐
- ☐
- ☐
- ☐
- ☐
- ☐
- ☐
- ☐
- ☐
- ☐
- ☐

## Wardrobe

- ☐ Safety Pins
- ☐ Sewing kit
- ☐ Small Scissors
- ☐ Lint Roller
- ☐ Fashion tape
- ☐ Steamer/iron
- ☐
- ☐
- ☐
- ☐
- ☐
- ☐
- ☐
- ☐
- ☐
- ☐
- ☐
- ☐
- ☐
- ☐
- ☐
- ☐
- ☐
- ☐

# Wedding Emergency Kit

| Other | Medical Kit | Notes |
|---|---|---|
| ☐ Cash | ☐ Sunscreen | _____ |
| ☐ Phone Charger | ☐ Band-aids | _____ |
| ☐ Razors | ☐ Pepto-Bismol | _____ |
| ☐ Tampons or Pads | ☐ Blister Balm | _____ |
| ☐ Drinking Straw | ☐ Antacids | _____ |
| ☐ Snacks | ☐ Pain reliever | _____ |
| ☐ Tissues | ☐ | _____ |
| ☐ Water | ☐ | _____ |
| ☐ Hand Sanitizer | ☐ | _____ |
| ☐ Stain remover | ☐ | _____ |
| ☐ Bug spray | ☐ | _____ |
| ☐ | ☐ | _____ |
| ☐ | ☐ | _____ |
| ☐ | ☐ | _____ |
| ☐ | ☐ | _____ |
| ☐ | ☐ | _____ |
| ☐ | ☐ | _____ |
| ☐ | ☐ | _____ |
| ☐ | ☐ | _____ |
| ☐ | ☐ | _____ |
| ☐ | ☐ | _____ |
| ☐ | ☐ | _____ |
| ☐ | ☐ | _____ |

Bridal Party

# Bridal shower Details

DATE:

TIME:

VENUE:

THEME:

ATTIRE:

## Games

## Food, Drinks & Decor

- [ ]
- [ ]
- [ ]
- [ ]
- [ ]
- [ ]
- [ ]
- [ ]
- [ ]
- [ ]
- [ ]
- [ ]
- [ ]
- [ ]
- [ ]
- [ ]
- [ ]
- [ ]
- [ ]
- [ ]
- [ ]
- [ ]
- [ ]
- [ ]

## To-Do List

- [ ]
- [ ]
- [ ]
- [ ]
- [ ]
- [ ]
- [ ]
- [ ]
- [ ]
- [ ]
- [ ]
- [ ]
- [ ]
- [ ]
- [ ]
- [ ]
- [ ]
- [ ]
- [ ]
- [ ]
- [ ]
- [ ]

| Time | Activities |
| --- | --- |
|  |  |
|  |  |
|  |  |
|  |  |
|  |  |

## Notes

# Guest list bridal shower

| Guest Name | Contact Number | Invitation Status | RSVP |
|---|---|---|---|
| | | | |
| | | | |
| | | | |
| | | | |
| | | | |
| | | | |
| | | | |
| | | | |
| | | | |
| | | | |
| | | | |
| | | | |
| | | | |
| | | | |
| | | | |
| | | | |
| | | | |
| | | | |
| | | | |
| | | | |
| | | | |
| | | | |
| | | | |
| | | | |
| | | | |
| | | | |
| | | | |
| | | | |

# Guest list bridal shower

| Guest Name | Contact Number | Invitation Status | RSVP |
|---|---|---|---|
| | | | |
| | | | |
| | | | |
| | | | |
| | | | |
| | | | |
| | | | |
| | | | |
| | | | |
| | | | |
| | | | |
| | | | |
| | | | |
| | | | |
| | | | |
| | | | |
| | | | |
| | | | |
| | | | |
| | | | |
| | | | |
| | | | |
| | | | |
| | | | |

# Bridal shower budget

| Expense | Budget | Deposit | Balance Due | Total Spend |
|---|---|---|---|---|
| Venue | | | | |
| Catering | | | | |
| Beverages | | | | |
| Alcohol | | | | |
| Flowers | | | | |
| Games | | | | |
| Table decorations | | | | |
| Thank you cards | | | | |
| Signs | | | | |
| Shipping Cost | | | | |
| | | | | |
| | | | | |
| | | | | |
| | | | | |
| | | | | |
| | | | | |
| | | | | |
| | | | | |
| | | | | |
| | | | | |
| | | | | |
| | | | | |
| | | | | |
| | | | | |
| | | | | |

# Bridal shower Timeline

## 3 Months Before

## 6 Weeks Before

## 1 Months Before

# Bridal shower Timeline

## 2 Weeks Before

## 1 Week Before

## On The Day

# Bridal Shower Tasks

| Name | Contact Number | Tasks & Responsibilities |
|------|----------------|--------------------------|
|      |                |                          |
|      |                |                          |
|      |                |                          |
|      |                |                          |
|      |                |                          |
|      |                |                          |
|      |                |                          |
|      |                |                          |
|      |                |                          |
|      |                |                          |
|      |                |                          |
|      |                |                          |
|      |                |                          |
|      |                |                          |
|      |                |                          |
|      |                |                          |
|      |                |                          |
|      |                |                          |
|      |                |                          |
|      |                |                          |
|      |                |                          |
|      |                |                          |

# Bachelorette party details

| DATE: | |
|---|---|
| TIME: | |
| VENUE: | |
| THEME: | |
| ATTIRE: | |

## Food, Drinks & Decor

- [ ]
- [ ]
- [ ]
- [ ]
- [ ]
- [ ]
- [ ]
- [ ]
- [ ]
- [ ]
- [ ]
- [ ]
- [ ]
- [ ]
- [ ]
- [ ]
- [ ]
- [ ]
- [ ]
- [ ]
- [ ]
- [ ]
- [ ]
- [ ]
- [ ]

## To-Do List

- [ ]
- [ ]
- [ ]
- [ ]
- [ ]
- [ ]
- [ ]
- [ ]
- [ ]
- [ ]
- [ ]
- [ ]
- [ ]
- [ ]
- [ ]
- [ ]
- [ ]
- [ ]
- [ ]
- [ ]
- [ ]

## Games

## Time | Activities

| Time | Activities |
|---|---|
| | |
| | |
| | |
| | |
| | |
| | |
| | |

## Notes

32

# Guest list bachelorette party

| Guest Name | Contact Number | Invitation Status | RSVP |
|---|---|---|---|
| | | | |
| | | | |
| | | | |
| | | | |
| | | | |
| | | | |
| | | | |
| | | | |
| | | | |
| | | | |
| | | | |
| | | | |
| | | | |
| | | | |
| | | | |
| | | | |
| | | | |
| | | | |
| | | | |
| | | | |
| | | | |
| | | | |
| | | | |
| | | | |
| | | | |
| | | | |

# Guest list bachelorette party

| Guest Name | Contact Number | Invitation Status | RSVP |
|---|---|---|---|
|  |  |  |  |
|  |  |  |  |
|  |  |  |  |
|  |  |  |  |
|  |  |  |  |
|  |  |  |  |
|  |  |  |  |
|  |  |  |  |
|  |  |  |  |
|  |  |  |  |
|  |  |  |  |
|  |  |  |  |
|  |  |  |  |
|  |  |  |  |
|  |  |  |  |
|  |  |  |  |
|  |  |  |  |
|  |  |  |  |
|  |  |  |  |
|  |  |  |  |
|  |  |  |  |
|  |  |  |  |
|  |  |  |  |
|  |  |  |  |
|  |  |  |  |
|  |  |  |  |

# Bachelorette party budget

| Expense | Budget | Deposit | Balance Due | Total Spend |
|---|---|---|---|---|
| Venue | | | | |
| Catering | | | | |
| Beverages | | | | |
| Alcohol | | | | |
| Flowers | | | | |
| Games | | | | |
| Table decorations | | | | |
| Thank you cards | | | | |
| Signs | | | | |
| Shipping Cost | | | | |
| | | | | |
| | | | | |
| | | | | |
| | | | | |
| | | | | |
| | | | | |
| | | | | |
| | | | | |
| | | | | |
| | | | | |
| | | | | |
| | | | | |
| | | | | |
| | | | | |

# Bachelorette party Timeline

## 3 Months Before

## 6 Weeks Before

## 1 Months Before

# Bachelorette party Timeline

## 2 Weeks Before

## 1 Week Before

## On The Day

# Bachelorette party duties

| Name | Contact Number | Tasks & Responsibilities |
|------|----------------|--------------------------|
|      |                |                          |
|      |                |                          |
|      |                |                          |
|      |                |                          |
|      |                |                          |
|      |                |                          |
|      |                |                          |
|      |                |                          |
|      |                |                          |
|      |                |                          |
|      |                |                          |
|      |                |                          |
|      |                |                          |
|      |                |                          |
|      |                |                          |
|      |                |                          |
|      |                |                          |
|      |                |                          |
|      |                |                          |
|      |                |                          |
|      |                |                          |
|      |                |                          |
|      |                |                          |
|      |                |                          |
|      |                |                          |

# Maid of honor attire

## Dress

PICK–UP DATE

SHOP_____

CONTACT DETAILS_____

ORDER DATE_____FITTING DATE_____

DRESS DETAILS_____

## Shoes and accessories

| Item | Details | Price | Received |
|------|---------|-------|----------|
|      |         |       |          |
|      |         |       |          |
|      |         |       |          |
|      |         |       |          |
|      |         |       |          |
|      |         |       |          |
|      |         |       |          |
|      |         |       |          |
|      |         |       |          |

## Notes

# Beauty Planner

## Makeup

| | |
|---|---|
| SALON | |
| MAKEUP ARTIST | |
| ADDRESS | |
| CONSULTATION | |
| DEPOSIT | |
| TOTAL COST | |

## Nails

| | |
|---|---|
| SALON | |
| CONTACT | |
| STYLE | |
| CONSULTATION | |
| DEPOSIT | |
| TOTAL COST | |

## Spa/ Other

| | |
|---|---|
| | |
| | |
| | |
| | |
| | |
| | |

## Hair

| | |
|---|---|
| HAIR STYLE | |
| SALON | |
| STYLIST | |
| STYLE IDEAS | |
| DEPOSIT | |
| TOTAL COST | |

## Appointment times

HAIR :                          MAKEUP:

NAILS :                         SPA :

# Bridesmaids attire

## Dresses

PICK-UP DATE

SHOP_____

CONTACT DETAILS_____

ORDER DATE_____ FITTING DATE_____

NOTES_____

| Size | Color | Who is wearing it? | Price | Notes |
|------|-------|-------------------|-------|-------|
|      |       |                   |       |       |
|      |       |                   |       |       |
|      |       |                   |       |       |
|      |       |                   |       |       |
|      |       |                   |       |       |
|      |       |                   |       |       |
|      |       |                   |       |       |
|      |       |                   |       |       |
|      |       |                   |       |       |
|      |       |                   |       |       |
|      |       |                   |       |       |
|      |       |                   |       |       |

## Notes

# Bridesmaids attire
## Shoes and accessories

| Who is wearing it? | Size | Color | Price | Notes |
|---|---|---|---|---|
| | | | | |
| | | | | |
| | | | | |
| | | | | |
| | | | | |
| | | | | |
| | | | | |
| | | | | |
| | | | | |
| | | | | |
| | | | | |
| | | | | |
| | | | | |
| | | | | |
| | | | | |
| | | | | |
| | | | | |
| | | | | |
| | | | | |
| | | | | |
| | | | | |
| | | | | |
| | | | | |
| | | | | |
| | | | | |
| | | | | |

# Monthly & Weekly Undated Planner

# January

| MON | TUE | WED | THU | FRI | SAT | SUN |
|-----|-----|-----|-----|-----|-----|-----|
|     |     |     |     |     |     |     |
|     |     |     |     |     |     |     |
|     |     |     |     |     |     |     |
|     |     |     |     |     |     |     |
|     |     |     |     |     |     |     |

## Notes

# February

| MON | TUE | WED | THU | FRI | SAT | SUN |
|-----|-----|-----|-----|-----|-----|-----|
|     |     |     |     |     |     |     |
|     |     |     |     |     |     |     |
|     |     |     |     |     |     |     |
|     |     |     |     |     |     |     |
|     |     |     |     |     |     |     |

## Notes

# March

| MON | TUE | WED | THU | FRI | SAT | SUN |
|-----|-----|-----|-----|-----|-----|-----|
|     |     |     |     |     |     |     |
|     |     |     |     |     |     |     |
|     |     |     |     |     |     |     |
|     |     |     |     |     |     |     |
|     |     |     |     |     |     |     |

## Notes

# April

| MON | TUE | WED | THU | FRI | SAT | SUN |
|-----|-----|-----|-----|-----|-----|-----|
|     |     |     |     |     |     |     |
|     |     |     |     |     |     |     |
|     |     |     |     |     |     |     |
|     |     |     |     |     |     |     |
|     |     |     |     |     |     |     |

## Notes

# May

| MON | TUE | WED | THU | FRI | SAT | SUN |
|-----|-----|-----|-----|-----|-----|-----|
|     |     |     |     |     |     |     |
|     |     |     |     |     |     |     |
|     |     |     |     |     |     |     |
|     |     |     |     |     |     |     |
|     |     |     |     |     |     |     |

## Notes

# June

| MON | TUE | WED | THU | FRI | SAT | SUN |
|-----|-----|-----|-----|-----|-----|-----|
|     |     |     |     |     |     |     |
|     |     |     |     |     |     |     |
|     |     |     |     |     |     |     |
|     |     |     |     |     |     |     |
|     |     |     |     |     |     |     |

## Notes

# July

| MON | TUE | WED | THU | FRI | SAT | SUN |
|-----|-----|-----|-----|-----|-----|-----|
|     |     |     |     |     |     |     |
|     |     |     |     |     |     |     |
|     |     |     |     |     |     |     |
|     |     |     |     |     |     |     |
|     |     |     |     |     |     |     |

## Notes

# August

| MON | TUE | WED | THU | FRI | SAT | SUN |
|-----|-----|-----|-----|-----|-----|-----|
|     |     |     |     |     |     |     |
|     |     |     |     |     |     |     |
|     |     |     |     |     |     |     |
|     |     |     |     |     |     |     |
|     |     |     |     |     |     |     |

## Notes

# September

| MON | TUE | WED | THU | FRI | SAT | SUN |
|-----|-----|-----|-----|-----|-----|-----|
|     |     |     |     |     |     |     |
|     |     |     |     |     |     |     |
|     |     |     |     |     |     |     |
|     |     |     |     |     |     |     |
|     |     |     |     |     |     |     |

## Notes

# October

| MON | TUE | WED | THU | FRI | SAT | SUN |
|-----|-----|-----|-----|-----|-----|-----|
|     |     |     |     |     |     |     |
|     |     |     |     |     |     |     |
|     |     |     |     |     |     |     |
|     |     |     |     |     |     |     |
|     |     |     |     |     |     |     |

## Notes

# November

| MON | TUE | WED | THU | FRI | SAT | SUN |
|-----|-----|-----|-----|-----|-----|-----|
|     |     |     |     |     |     |     |
|     |     |     |     |     |     |     |
|     |     |     |     |     |     |     |
|     |     |     |     |     |     |     |
|     |     |     |     |     |     |     |

## Notes

# December

| MON | TUE | WED | THU | FRI | SAT | SUN |
|-----|-----|-----|-----|-----|-----|-----|
|     |     |     |     |     |     |     |
|     |     |     |     |     |     |     |
|     |     |     |     |     |     |     |
|     |     |     |     |     |     |     |
|     |     |     |     |     |     |     |

## Notes

# Weekly planner

| | |
|---|---|
| **MONDAY** | |
| **TUESDAY** | |
| **WEDNESDAY** | |
| **THURSDAY** | |
| **FRIDAY** | |
| **SATURDAY** | |
| **SUNDAY** | |

## TOP PRIORITIES

........................................................
........................................................
........................................................
........................................................
........................................................
........................................................
........................................................

## TO DO LIST

## NOTES

........................................................
........................................................
........................................................
........................................................
........................................................

## APPOINTMENTS

♥
♥
♥
♥
♥
♥
♥
♥

# Weekly planner

| | |
|---|---|
| **MONDAY** | |
| **TUESDAY** | |
| **WEDNESDAY** | |
| **THURSDAY** | |
| **FRIDAY** | |
| **SATURDAY** | |
| **SUNDAY** | |

### TOP PRIORITIES

............................................................
............................................................
............................................................
............................................................
............................................................
............................................................
............................................................

### TO DO LIST

### NOTES

............................................................
............................................................
............................................................
............................................................
............................................................
............................................................

### APPOINTMENTS

♥
♥
♥
♥
♥
♥
♥
♥

# Weekly planner

| | |
|---|---|
| **MONDAY** | |
| **TUESDAY** | |
| **WEDNESDAY** | |
| **THURSDAY** | |
| **FRIDAY** | |
| **SATURDAY** | |
| **SUNDAY** | |

## TOP PRIORITIES

........................................................
........................................................
........................................................
........................................................
........................................................
........................................................

## TO DO LIST

## NOTES

........................................................
........................................................
........................................................
........................................................
........................................................

## APPOINTMENTS

♥
♥
♥
♥
♥
♥
♥
♥

# Weekly planner

| | |
|---|---|
| **MONDAY** | |
| **TUESDAY** | |
| **WEDNESDAY** | |
| **THURSDAY** | |
| **FRIDAY** | |
| **SATURDAY** | |
| **SUNDAY** | |

## TOP PRIORITIES

........................................................
........................................................
........................................................
........................................................
........................................................
........................................................

## TO DO LIST

## NOTES

........................................................
........................................................
........................................................
........................................................
........................................................

## APPOINTMENTS

♥
♥
♥
♥
♥
♥
♥
♥

# Weekly planner

| | |
|---|---|
| **MONDAY** | |
| **TUESDAY** | |
| **WEDNESDAY** | |
| **THURSDAY** | |
| **FRIDAY** | |
| **SATURDAY** | |
| **SUNDAY** | |

### TOP PRIORITIES

......................................................
......................................................
......................................................
......................................................
......................................................
......................................................

### TO DO LIST

### NOTES

......................................................
......................................................
......................................................
......................................................
......................................................

### APPOINTMENTS

♥
♥
♥
♥
♥
♥
♥
♥

# Weekly planner

| | |
|---|---|
| MONDAY | |
| TUESDAY | |
| WEDNESDAY | |
| THURSDAY | |
| FRIDAY | |
| SATURDAY | |
| SUNDAY | |

## TOP PRIORITIES

...................................................
...................................................
...................................................
...................................................
...................................................
...................................................
...................................................

## TO DO LIST

## NOTES

...................................................
...................................................
...................................................
...................................................
...................................................
...................................................

## APPOINTMENTS

♥
♥
♥
♥
♥
♥
♥
♥

# Weekly planner

| | |
|---|---|
| **MONDAY** | |
| **TUESDAY** | |
| **WEDNESDAY** | |
| **THURSDAY** | |
| **FRIDAY** | |
| **SATURDAY** | |
| **SUNDAY** | |

## TOP PRIORITIES

........................................................
........................................................
........................................................
........................................................
........................................................
........................................................

## TO DO LIST

## NOTES

........................................................
........................................................
........................................................
........................................................
........................................................

## APPOINTMENTS

♥
♥
♥
♥
♥
♥
♥
♥
♥

# Weekly planner

| | |
|---|---|
| **MONDAY** | |
| **TUESDAY** | |
| **WEDNESDAY** | |
| **THURSDAY** | |
| **FRIDAY** | |
| **SATURDAY** | |
| **SUNDAY** | |

## TOP PRIORITIES

........................................................

........................................................

........................................................

........................................................

........................................................

........................................................

........................................................

## TO DO LIST

## NOTES

........................................................

........................................................

........................................................

........................................................

........................................................

## APPOINTMENTS

♥
♥
♥
♥
♥
♥
♥
♥

# Weekly planner

| | |
|---|---|
| **MONDAY** | |
| **TUESDAY** | |
| **WEDNESDAY** | |
| **THURSDAY** | |
| **FRIDAY** | |
| **SATURDAY** | |
| **SUNDAY** | |

## TOP PRIORITIES

## TO DO LIST

## NOTES

## APPOINTMENTS

♥
♥
♥
♥
♥
♥
♥
♥

# Weekly planner

**MONDAY**

**TUESDAY**

**WEDNESDAY**

**THURSDAY**

**FRIDAY**

**SATURDAY**

**SUNDAY**

## TOP PRIORITIES

........................................................
........................................................
........................................................
........................................................
........................................................
........................................................
........................................................

## TO DO LIST

## NOTES

........................................................
........................................................
........................................................
........................................................
........................................................

## APPOINTMENTS

♥
♥
♥
♥
♥
♥
♥
♥

# Weekly planner

| | |
|---|---|
| **MONDAY** | |
| **TUESDAY** | |
| **WEDNESDAY** | |
| **THURSDAY** | |
| **FRIDAY** | |
| **SATURDAY** | |
| **SUNDAY** | |

## TOP PRIORITIES

........................................................
........................................................
........................................................
........................................................
........................................................
........................................................
........................................................

## TO DO LIST

## NOTES

........................................................
........................................................
........................................................
........................................................
........................................................

## APPOINTMENTS

♥
♥
♥
♥
♥
♥
♥
♥
♥

# Weekly planner

| | |
|---|---|
| **MONDAY** | |
| **TUESDAY** | |
| **WEDNESDAY** | |
| **THURSDAY** | |
| **FRIDAY** | |
| **SATURDAY** | |
| **SUNDAY** | |

## TOP PRIORITIES

........................................................
........................................................
........................................................
........................................................
........................................................
........................................................
........................................................

## TO DO LIST

## NOTES

........................................................
........................................................
........................................................
........................................................
........................................................
........................................................

## APPOINTMENTS

♥
♥
♥
♥
♥
♥
♥
♥

# Weekly planner

| | |
|---|---|
| **MONDAY** | |
| **TUESDAY** | |
| **WEDNESDAY** | |
| **THURSDAY** | |
| **FRIDAY** | |
| **SATURDAY** | |
| **SUNDAY** | |

## TOP PRIORITIES

........................................................
........................................................
........................................................
........................................................
........................................................
........................................................
........................................................

## TO DO LIST

## NOTES

........................................................
........................................................
........................................................
........................................................
........................................................
........................................................

## APPOINTMENTS

♥
♥
♥
♥
♥
♥
♥
♥
♥

# Weekly planner

| | |
|---|---|
| **MONDAY** | |
| **TUESDAY** | |
| **WEDNESDAY** | |
| **THURSDAY** | |
| **FRIDAY** | |
| **SATURDAY** | |
| **SUNDAY** | |

### TOP PRIORITIES

### TO DO LIST

### NOTES

### APPOINTMENTS

# Weekly planner

| | |
|---|---|
| **MONDAY** | |
| **TUESDAY** | |
| **WEDNESDAY** | |
| **THURSDAY** | |
| **FRIDAY** | |
| **SATURDAY** | |
| **SUNDAY** | |

## TOP PRIORITIES

## TO DO LIST

## NOTES

## APPOINTMENTS

# Weekly planner

| | |
|---|---|
| **MONDAY** | |
| **TUESDAY** | |
| **WEDNESDAY** | |
| **THURSDAY** | |
| **FRIDAY** | |
| **SATURDAY** | |
| **SUNDAY** | |

### TOP PRIORITIES

### TO DO LIST

### NOTES

### APPOINTMENTS

# Weekly planner

| | |
|---|---|
| MONDAY | |
| TUESDAY | |
| WEDNESDAY | |
| THURSDAY | |
| FRIDAY | |
| SATURDAY | |
| SUNDAY | |

## TOP PRIORITIES

...............................................
...............................................
...............................................
...............................................
...............................................
...............................................

## TO DO LIST

## NOTES

...............................................
...............................................
...............................................
...............................................
...............................................

## APPOINTMENTS

♥
♥
♥
♥
♥
♥
♥
♥
♥

# Weekly planner

| | |
|---|---|
| **MONDAY** | |
| **TUESDAY** | |
| **WEDNESDAY** | |
| **THURSDAY** | |
| **FRIDAY** | |
| **SATURDAY** | |
| **SUNDAY** | |

## TOP PRIORITIES

........................................................
........................................................
........................................................
........................................................
........................................................
........................................................
........................................................

## TO DO LIST

## NOTES

........................................................
........................................................
........................................................
........................................................
........................................................
........................................................

## APPOINTMENTS

♥
♥
♥
♥
♥
♥
♥

# Weekly planner

| | |
|---|---|
| **MONDAY** | |
| **TUESDAY** | |
| **WEDNESDAY** | |
| **THURSDAY** | |
| **FRIDAY** | |
| **SATURDAY** | |
| **SUNDAY** | |

## TOP PRIORITIES

........................................................
........................................................
........................................................
........................................................
........................................................
........................................................

## TO DO LIST

## NOTES

........................................................
........................................................
........................................................
........................................................
........................................................

## APPOINTMENTS

♥
♥
♥
♥
♥
♥
♥
♥

# Weekly planner

| | |
|---|---|
| **MONDAY** | |
| **TUESDAY** | |
| **WEDNESDAY** | |
| **THURSDAY** | |
| **FRIDAY** | |
| **SATURDAY** | |
| **SUNDAY** | |

## TOP PRIORITIES

## TO DO LIST

## NOTES

## APPOINTMENTS

♥
♥
♥
♥
♥
♥
♥
♥

# Weekly planner

| | |
|---|---|
| **MONDAY** | |
| **TUESDAY** | |
| **WEDNESDAY** | |
| **THURSDAY** | |
| **FRIDAY** | |
| **SATURDAY** | |
| **SUNDAY** | |

## TOP PRIORITIES

........................................................
........................................................
........................................................
........................................................
........................................................
........................................................
........................................................

## TO DO LIST

## NOTES

........................................................
........................................................
........................................................
........................................................
........................................................

## APPOINTMENTS

♥
♥
♥
♥
♥
♥
♥
♥
♥

# Weekly planner

| | |
|---|---|
| **MONDAY** | |
| **TUESDAY** | |
| **WEDNESDAY** | |
| **THURSDAY** | |
| **FRIDAY** | |
| **SATURDAY** | |
| **SUNDAY** | |

## TOP PRIORITIES

..........................................................
..........................................................
..........................................................
..........................................................
..........................................................
..........................................................
..........................................................

## TO DO LIST

## NOTES

..........................................................
..........................................................
..........................................................
..........................................................
..........................................................
..........................................................

## APPOINTMENTS

♥
♥
♥
♥
♥
♥
♥
♥
♥

# Weekly planner

| | |
|---|---|
| **MONDAY** | |
| **TUESDAY** | |
| **WEDNESDAY** | |
| **THURSDAY** | |
| **FRIDAY** | |
| **SATURDAY** | |
| **SUNDAY** | |

## TOP PRIORITIES

........................................................
........................................................
........................................................
........................................................
........................................................
........................................................
........................................................

## TO DO LIST

## NOTES

........................................................
........................................................
........................................................
........................................................
........................................................
........................................................

## APPOINTMENTS

♥
♥
♥
♥
♥
♥
♥
♥
♥

# Weekly planner

| | |
|---|---|
| **MONDAY** | |
| **TUESDAY** | |
| **WEDNESDAY** | |
| **THURSDAY** | |
| **FRIDAY** | |
| **SATURDAY** | |
| **SUNDAY** | |

## TOP PRIORITIES

........................................................
........................................................
........................................................
........................................................
........................................................
........................................................
........................................................

## TO DO LIST

## NOTES

........................................................
........................................................
........................................................
........................................................
........................................................
........................................................

## APPOINTMENTS

♥
♥
♥
♥
♥
♥
♥
♥

# Weekly planner

| | |
|---|---|
| **MONDAY** | |
| **TUESDAY** | |
| **WEDNESDAY** | |
| **THURSDAY** | |
| **FRIDAY** | |
| **SATURDAY** | |
| **SUNDAY** | |

## TOP PRIORITIES

..................................................
..................................................
..................................................
..................................................
..................................................
..................................................
..................................................

## TO DO LIST

## NOTES

..................................................
..................................................
..................................................
..................................................
..................................................

## APPOINTMENTS

♥
♥
♥
♥
♥
♥
♥
♥

# Weekly planner

| | |
|---|---|
| **MONDAY** | |
| **TUESDAY** | |
| **WEDNESDAY** | |
| **THURSDAY** | |
| **FRIDAY** | |
| **SATURDAY** | |
| **SUNDAY** | |

## TOP PRIORITIES

..............................................................
..............................................................
..............................................................
..............................................................
..............................................................
..............................................................
..............................................................

## TO DO LIST

## NOTES

..............................................................
..............................................................
..............................................................
..............................................................
..............................................................
..............................................................

## APPOINTMENTS

♥
♥
♥
♥
♥
♥
♥
♥

# Weekly planner

| | |
|---|---|
| MONDAY | |
| TUESDAY | |
| WEDNESDAY | |
| THURSDAY | |
| FRIDAY | |
| SATURDAY | |
| SUNDAY | |

## TOP PRIORITIES

## TO DO LIST

## NOTES

## APPOINTMENTS

# Weekly planner

| | |
|---|---|
| **MONDAY** | |
| **TUESDAY** | |
| **WEDNESDAY** | |
| **THURSDAY** | |
| **FRIDAY** | |
| **SATURDAY** | |
| **SUNDAY** | |

### TOP PRIORITIES

........................................................
........................................................
........................................................
........................................................
........................................................
........................................................

### TO DO LIST

### NOTES

........................................................
........................................................
........................................................
........................................................
........................................................
........................................................

### APPOINTMENTS

♥
♥
♥
♥
♥
♥
♥
♥

# Weekly planner

| | |
|---|---|
| **MONDAY** | |
| **TUESDAY** | |
| **WEDNESDAY** | |
| **THURSDAY** | |
| **FRIDAY** | |
| **SATURDAY** | |
| **SUNDAY** | |

## TOP PRIORITIES

## TO DO LIST

## NOTES

## APPOINTMENTS

# Weekly planner

| | |
|---|---|
| **MONDAY** | |
| **TUESDAY** | |
| **WEDNESDAY** | |
| **THURSDAY** | |
| **FRIDAY** | |
| **SATURDAY** | |
| **SUNDAY** | |

## TOP PRIORITIES

........................................................
........................................................
........................................................
........................................................
........................................................
........................................................
........................................................

## TO DO LIST

## NOTES

........................................................
........................................................
........................................................
........................................................
........................................................

## APPOINTMENTS

♥
♥
♥
♥
♥
♥
♥
♥
♥

# Weekly planner

| | |
|---|---|
| **MONDAY** | |
| **TUESDAY** | |
| **WEDNESDAY** | |
| **THURSDAY** | |
| **FRIDAY** | |
| **SATURDAY** | |
| **SUNDAY** | |

## TOP PRIORITIES

........................................................
........................................................
........................................................
........................................................
........................................................
........................................................
........................................................

## TO DO LIST

## NOTES

........................................................
........................................................
........................................................
........................................................
........................................................

## APPOINTMENTS

♥
♥
♥
♥
♥
♥
♥
♥

# Wedding Toast

START PLANNING YOUR SPEECH ONE OR TWO MONTHS IN ADVANCE.
LET A FRIEND PROOFREAD IT.

## Speech Outline

- [x] HOW YOU KNOW THE BRIDE
- [x] FUNNY STORIES THAT ARE NOT EMBARRASSING
- [x] A SENTIMENTAL STORY FROM THE PAST
- [x] STORY ABOUT THE COUPLE: HOW THEY MET, HOW THEIR RELATIONSHIP BLOSSOMED OR WHAT MAKES THEM A PERFECT COUPLE
- [x] BEST WISHES FOR THE COUPLE
- [x] INVITE THE GUESTS TO RAISE THEIR GLASS

## Avoid

- [x] DO NOT BRING UP VERY EMBARRASSING STORIES
- [x] DO NOT USE SWEAR WORDS
- [x] DO NOT MENTION EX-BOYFRIENDS OR EX-HUSBANDS

# Wedding Toast Template

## INTRODUCE YOURSELF

## HUMOR

## THE BRIDE

## THE GROOM

## THE COUPLE

## HUMOR

## TOAST

# Online order tracker

| Date | Website/store | Item | Price | Shipped | Received |
|------|---------------|------|-------|---------|----------|
|      |               |      |       |         |          |
|      |               |      |       |         |          |
|      |               |      |       |         |          |
|      |               |      |       |         |          |
|      |               |      |       |         |          |
|      |               |      |       |         |          |
|      |               |      |       |         |          |
|      |               |      |       |         |          |
|      |               |      |       |         |          |
|      |               |      |       |         |          |
|      |               |      |       |         |          |
|      |               |      |       |         |          |
|      |               |      |       |         |          |
|      |               |      |       |         |          |
|      |               |      |       |         |          |
|      |               |      |       |         |          |
|      |               |      |       |         |          |
|      |               |      |       |         |          |
|      |               |      |       |         |          |
|      |               |      |       |         |          |
|      |               |      |       |         |          |
|      |               |      |       |         |          |
|      |               |      |       |         |          |
|      |               |      |       |         |          |

# Online order tracker

| Date | Website/store | Item | Price | Shipped | Received |
|------|---------------|------|-------|---------|----------|
|      |               |      |       |         |          |
|      |               |      |       |         |          |
|      |               |      |       |         |          |
|      |               |      |       |         |          |
|      |               |      |       |         |          |
|      |               |      |       |         |          |
|      |               |      |       |         |          |
|      |               |      |       |         |          |
|      |               |      |       |         |          |
|      |               |      |       |         |          |
|      |               |      |       |         |          |
|      |               |      |       |         |          |
|      |               |      |       |         |          |
|      |               |      |       |         |          |
|      |               |      |       |         |          |
|      |               |      |       |         |          |
|      |               |      |       |         |          |
|      |               |      |       |         |          |
|      |               |      |       |         |          |
|      |               |      |       |         |          |
|      |               |      |       |         |          |
|      |               |      |       |         |          |
|      |               |      |       |         |          |
|      |               |      |       |         |          |
|      |               |      |       |         |          |
|      |               |      |       |         |          |

# Tasks

| Tasks | Due Date | Done |
|---|---|---|
|  |  |  |
|  |  |  |
|  |  |  |
|  |  |  |
|  |  |  |
|  |  |  |
|  |  |  |
|  |  |  |
|  |  |  |
|  |  |  |
|  |  |  |
|  |  |  |
|  |  |  |
|  |  |  |
|  |  |  |
|  |  |  |
|  |  |  |
|  |  |  |
|  |  |  |
|  |  |  |
|  |  |  |
|  |  |  |
|  |  |  |
|  |  |  |

# Tasks

| Tasks | Due Date | Done |
|---|---|---|
| | | |
| | | |
| | | |
| | | |
| | | |
| | | |
| | | |
| | | |
| | | |
| | | |
| | | |
| | | |
| | | |
| | | |
| | | |
| | | |
| | | |
| | | |
| | | |
| | | |
| | | |
| | | |
| | | |
| | | |
| | | |

# Notes

# Notes

# Notes

# Notes

# Notes

_____
_____
_____
_____
_____
_____
_____
_____
_____
_____
_____
_____
_____
_____
_____
_____
_____
_____
_____
_____
_____
_____
_____
_____

# Notes

_____

_____

_____

_____

_____

_____

_____

_____

_____

_____

_____

_____

_____

_____

_____

_____

_____

_____

_____

_____

_____

_____

_____

# Notes

# Notes

# Wedding day schedule

| Time | Schedule |
|------|----------|
|      |          |
|      |          |
|      |          |
|      |          |
|      |          |
|      |          |
|      |          |
|      |          |
|      |          |
|      |          |
|      |          |
|      |          |
|      |          |
|      |          |
|      |          |
|      |          |
|      |          |
|      |          |
|      |          |
|      |          |
|      |          |
|      |          |
|      |          |
|      |          |

# Bridal shower Memories

# Bachelorette Memories

# Wedding Memories

# My favourite picture

Printed in Great Britain
by Amazon

27449461R00059